QUICK REVISION NOTES -PART I (BIOLOGY)

QUICK LEARNING NOTES FOR EXAMS NCERT BASED (BONUS-QUESTIONS AND ANSWERS)-PART I (UNIT I)

MONICA SHARMA

Made with ♥ on the Notion Press Platform
www.notionpress.com

Contents

Preface

Introducing the ultimate guide for CBSE exam preparation - CBSE Notes and Question Bank Book! This comprehensive guide is designed to help students in their preparation for the CBSE board exams. The book contains a comprehensive collection of notes, and questions-answers for Biology subject for Class 11.

This book has been specifically designed to meet the needs of CBSE students preparing for their board exams. The notes in this book are concise and well-organized, making it easier for students to understand the concepts and remember them for a longer time. Each chapter in the book contains detailed notes that cover all the important topics and concepts. The book also includes a comprehensive collection of questions that cover all types of questions that can be asked in the CBSE board exams. This book is an invaluable resource for CBSE students as it not only helps them prepare for the board exams but also helps them understand the subject in-depth, making it easier for them to score well in the exams. The book is written in an easy-to-understand language, making it accessible to all students, regardless of their proficiency level.

In summary, CBSE Notes and Question Bank Book is an essential resource for CBSE students who want to score high marks in their board exams. With its comprehensive coverage of notes and questions, this book is an all-in-one guide that will help students achieve their academic goals. Get your copy today and get started on your path to success! Part II, III, IV, and V for the other 4 units of Biology Class 11 NCERT is also available at 39/- per Part.

For Booking your Copy Contact: ms.bioacademy@gmail.com

Prologue

Part -I

CBSE Class 11th NCERT Based Notes For Quick Revision in Exams
Question Bank
Unit – I of NCERT Biology Class 11th Book
Includes Chapter-1 : The living World
Chapter-2 : Biological Classification
Chapter-3 : Plant Kingdom
Chapter-4 : Animal Kingdom

CHAPTER ONE

Chapter 1 "The Living World"

Definition of Biology: Biology is the study of living organisms and their relationship with the environment.

Characteristics of living organisms: All living organisms are characterized by seven common properties, including growth and development, reproduction, response to stimuli, homeostasis, energy utilization, evolution, and adaptation.

Diversity of Living Organisms: The living world is incredibly diverse, with over 1.5 million species of plants and animals, and even more microorganisms.

Taxonomy: Taxonomy is the study of the classification of living organisms into various groups based on their similarities and differences. It helps to understand the diversity of living organisms and their evolutionary relationships.

Binomial Nomenclature: Binomial Nomenclature is a system of naming living organisms, consisting of two Latin words, the first representing the genus and the second the species.

Five Kingdom Classification: The Five Kingdom classification system categorizes living organisms into Monera, Protista, Fungi, Plantae, and Animalia based on their characteristics and evolutionary relationships.

Biodiversity: Biodiversity refers to the variety of life forms, genes, and ecosystems in a given region. It plays a crucial role in maintaining the balance of the ecosystem and provides numerous benefits to humans.

Endangered Species: Endangered species are those that are in danger of extinction due to habitat loss, over-exploitation, and other factors. Conservation efforts are needed to protect these species and preserve biodiversity.

Conservation of Biodiversity: Conservation of biodiversity refers to the protection and preservation of biodiversity in its natural state. It involves the protection of habitats, reducing pollution and habitat destruction, and regulating the exploitation of natural resources.

Biosphere: The biosphere is the part of the earth where life exists. It is composed of all the living organisms and their physical environment, including air, water, and soil.

Ecosystem: An ecosystem is a community of living and non-living things that interact with each other. It includes all the living organisms, their physical and chemical environment, and the relationships between them.

Ecological Interactions: Ecological interactions refer to the relationships between living organisms and their environment. These interactions can be categorized into mutualism, commensalism, parasitism, and competition.

Food Chains and Food Webs: Food chains and food webs are diagrams that show the transfer of energy from one organism to another in an ecosystem. They demonstrate how energy is transformed from one form to another, and how all living organisms are interconnected in the ecosystem.

Biogeochemical Cycles: Biogeochemical cycles refer to the movement of chemical elements and compounds through the biosphere, atmosphere, hydrosphere, and geosphere. The carbon, nitrogen, and phosphorus cycles are the most important biogeochemical cycles in the ecosystem.

Biotic Potential and Environmental Resistance: Biotic potential refers to the maximum growth rate of a population under ideal conditions, while environmental resistance refers to the factors that limit the growth of a population. The balance between biotic potential and environmental resistance determines the size and stability of a population.

CHAPTER TWO

Chapter 2 Biological Classification

Biological Classification is a fundamental organizer and a systematic way of understanding the diversity of life on Earth.

Introduction: Biological classification is the process of organizing living organisms into categories based on their similarities and differences. This helps in understanding the diversity of life on Earth and their evolutionary relationships.

Need for Classification: The need for classification arises from the large number of species on Earth and the need to study and understand them in a systematic manner. It also helps in naming and identifying species and in communicating scientific information about them.

Taxonomy: Taxonomy is the science of classification that involves the identification, naming, and classification of living organisms.

Binomial Nomenclature: Binomial Nomenclature is a system of naming living organisms that consists of *two Latin words*, the first representing *the genus and the second the species*. This system of naming was introduced by **Carl Linnaeus.**

Hierarchical Classification: Hierarchical classification is a system of classification that categorizes living organisms into increasingly specific groups based on their characteristics. The main categories of hierarchical classification are Kingdom, Phylum, Class, Order, Family, Genus, and Species.

Five Kingdom Classification: The Five Kingdom classification system categorizes living organisms into Monera, Protista, Fungi, Plantae, and Animalia based on their similarities and differences.

1. **Characteristics of Monera:** Monera are unicellular organisms that lack a nucleus and other membrane-bound organelles. They are further divided into two groups: Prokaryotes (bacteria) and Cyanobacteria (blue-green algae).
2. **Characteristics of Protista**: Protista are unicellular or colonial organisms that possess a nucleus and other membrane-bound organelles. They are the simplest form of eukaryotes and are found in various environments, including freshwater and marine habitats.
3. **Characteristics of Fungi:** Fungi are multicellular organisms that lack chlorophyll and obtain their food by absorbing nutrients from other living or dead organisms. They play an important role in the ecosystem by breaking down dead organic matter and recycling nutrients.
4. **Characteristics of Plantae:** Plantae are multicellular organisms that possess chlorophyll and are capable of photosynthesis. They are further divided into vascular and non-vascular plants.
5. **Characteristics of Animalia:** Animalia are multicellular organisms that lack chlorophyll and obtain their food by consuming other organisms. They are further divided into invertebrates and vertebrates based on their body plan and the presence or absence of a backbone.

It is important to note that biological classification is not a static process and it is subject to change as new information and discoveries are made. The classification of organisms is based on multiple criteria such as morphological, molecular, and physiological characteristics. These criteria are used to determine the evolutionary relationships between different species and the classification of each species within the hierarchy of taxonomic groups.

The process of biological classification has also been greatly aided by the development of molecular biology and DNA sequencing. These techniques have allowed scientists to analyze the genetic makeup of organisms and determine their evolutionary relationships more accurately.

The Five Kingdom classification system categorizes living organisms into Monera, Protista, Fungi, Plantae, and Animalia based on their similarities and differences. Here are the main characteristics of each kingdom:

- **Monera:**

- Unicellular organisms
- Lack a nucleus and other membrane-bound organelles
- Prokaryotes (bacteria) and Cyanobacteria (blue-green algae)

- **Protista:**

- Unicellular or colonial organisms
- Possess a nucleus and other membrane-bound organelles
- Found in various environments, including freshwater and marine habitats

- **Fungi:**
- Multicellular organisms
- Lack chlorophyll and obtain their food by absorbing nutrients from other living or dead organisms
- Play an important role in the ecosystem by breaking down dead organic matter and recycling nutrients

- **Plantae:**

- Multicellular organisms
- Possess chlorophyll and are capable of photosynthesis
- Further divided into vascular and non-vascular plants

- **Animalia:**

- Multicellular organisms
- Lack chlorophyll and obtain their food by consuming other organisms
- Further divided into invertebrates and vertebrates based on their body plan and the presence or absence of a backbone

Extra Bites...

Kingdom Monera is one of the five kingdoms in the Five Kingdom classification system that categorizes living organisms based on their similarities and differences. Here are some key notes on Kingdom Monera:

1. Prokaryotic organisms: Kingdom Monera consists of prokaryotic organisms, which are unicellular organisms that lack a nucleus and other membrane-bound organelles.
2. Bacterial species: The most well-known members of Kingdom Monera are bacteria, which are single-celled organisms that can be found in a variety of environments, including soil, water, and the human gut.
3. Cyanobacteria: Kingdom Monera also includes Cyanobacteria, commonly known as blue-green algae, which are photosynthetic bacteria that produce oxygen and play a crucial role in the Earth's atmosphere.

4. Diversity: Despite their simple structure, bacteria are incredibly diverse and show a wide range of metabolic diversity, allowing them to thrive in a variety of environments, including extreme conditions such as high temperatures and high salt concentrations.
5. Ecological significance: Bacteria play a crucial role in the ecosystem by breaking down organic matter and recycling nutrients, as well as playing a role in nitrogen fixation, which is the process of converting atmospheric nitrogen into a form that can be used by plants.
6. Importance in medicine and industry: Bacteria are also important in medicine and industry, with many species being used in the production of antibiotics and other important compounds, as well as in bioremediation, which is the use of microorganisms to clean up contaminated environments.

Archaebacteria and Eubacteria are two major groups of bacteria that differ in their evolutionary history, metabolic processes, and cell structure.

1. **Archaebacteria:**

- Distinct evolutionary lineage from eubacteria
- Usually found in extreme environments, such as hot springs, salt lakes, and deep-sea vents
- Unique cell structure, including a different type of cell membrane and a different type of ribosome
- Metabolic processes that are different from those of eubacteria, including the use of methanogenesis, a process of generating energy from methane, as a means of survival in extreme environments

1. **Eubacteria:**

- More closely related to eukaryotic organisms
- Found in a variety of environments, including soil, water, and the human gut
- Characterized by a simpler cell structure compared to eukaryotic organisms, lacking membrane-bound organelles such as the nucleus
- Metabolic processes that include respiration, photosynthesis, and fermentation

CHAPTER THREE

Chapter-3 Plant Kingdom

Plant Kingdom:

1. **Introduction:**

- Plant Kingdom refers to a diverse group of organisms that include all types of plants, from mosses to redwoods.
- The study of plants is called botany.

1. **Characteristics:**

- Multicellular and photosynthetic
- Cell walls made of cellulose
- Autotrophic nutrition
- Reproduction through spores, spores, seeds or spores.

3. **Types of plants:**

- Non-vascular plants (mosses, liverworts)
- Vascular plants (ferns, gymnosperms, and angiosperms)

4. **Classification of Plants:**

- Based on presence or absence of seeds
    - Bryophytes (mosses, liverworts)
    - Pteridophytes (ferns)
    - Gymnosperms (conifers)
    - Angiosperms (flowering plants)
- Based on vascular system:
    - Non-vascular plants
    - Vascular plants

5. **Importance of plants:**

- Providing oxygen and food through photosynthesis
- Maintaining the balance of atmospheric gases

- Soil conservation
- Source of medicines and industrial products.

<u>**Classification:**</u>

Plant Kingdom Classification:

1. **Introduction:**

- The classification of plants is based on various morphological, anatomical, and physiological characteristics.
- It helps in understanding the evolutionary relationships among different types of plants and provides a basis for their identification and study.

2. **Historical classification:**

- The earliest classification of plants was based on simple morphological features, such as the presence or absence of seeds and leaves.
- As knowledge of plant anatomy and physiology advanced, more sophisticated methods of classification were developed.

3. **Modern classification:**

- Modern classification is based on the Linnaean system, which categorizes plants into different taxa (classes, orders, families, genera, and species).
- The classification is hierarchical, with each taxon being a subset of the taxon above it.

4. **Major classification systems:**

- Based on the presence or absence of seeds:
    - Bryophytes (mosses, liverworts)
    - Pteridophytes (ferns)
    - Gymnosperms (conifers)
    - Angiosperms (flowering plants)
- Based on the vascular system:
    - Non-vascular plants
    - Vascular plants
-

5. **Key features used in classification:**

- Presence or absence of seeds, leaves, and stems
- Presence or absence of a vascular system
- Reproduction methods (e.g., spores, spores, seeds or spores)
- Structure of flowers and fruits
- Chromosome numbers
- Chemical and molecular characteristics

Characteristics of plant Kingdom classification:

v. **Thallophyte:**

1. Introduction:

- They were traditionally called simple plants or thalloid plants or lower plants and belonged to a polyphyletic group of non-motile organisms.

2. Characteristics:

- They lack stems, roots, or leaves.
- They are mainly found in damp areas.
- They are autotrophic in nature.
- They lack a vascular system.
- Most thallophytes have cellulose in their cell walls.
- Mostly their reproductive organs contain a single cell and are simple.

3. Examples:

- Ulothrix, Spirogyra, Cladophora and Chara

v. **Pteridophyte:**

1. Introduction:

- Pteridophytes are a group of vascular plants that reproduce through spores, spores and seeds.
- They are characterized by their unique leaves and stems, and a complex root system.

2. Characteristics:

- Vascular system (xylem and phloem)
- Complex roots
- Reproduction through spores, spores and seeds
- Sporophyte stage is dominant

3. Examples:

- Ferns, horsetails, and whisk ferns
- Typically found in moist environments such as forests, swamps, and near water sources.

4. Importance:

- They play a crucial role in the ecosystem, serving as food for many animals and insects.
- They also provide habitat and shelter for many species.

v. **Bryophyte:**

1. Introduction:

- Bryophytes are a group of non-vascular plants that include mosses, liverworts, and hornworts.
- They are characterized by their simple structure and method of reproduction.

2. Characteristics:

- No vascular system
- Simple structure (no true roots, stems, or leaves)
- Reproduction through spores
- Gametophyte stage is dominant

3. Examples:

- Mosses, liverworts, and hornworts
- Typically found in moist environments such as forests, swamps, and near water sources.

4. Importance:

- They play an important role in soil conservation by preventing erosion and enriching soil.
- They also provide habitat and shelter for many species of insects and animals.

v. **Gymnosperm:**

1. Introduction:

- Gymnosperms are a group of vascular plants that have seeds but do not have fruits.
- They are characterized by their naked seeds, which are not enclosed in an ovary.

2. Characteristics:

- Vascular system (xylem and phloem)
- Seeds are not enclosed in an ovary
- Reproduction through seeds
- Cones are the reproductive structures

3. Examples:

- Conifers, cycads, and ginkgos
- Typically found in temperate regions, but some species are found in tropical regions.

4. Importance:

- They play a crucial role in the ecosystem, serving as food for many animals and insects.
- They also provide habitat and shelter for many species.
- Wood from gymnosperms is used for construction, paper production, and fuel.

v. **Angiosperm:**

1. Introduction:

- Angiosperms are a group of flowering plants that have seeds enclosed in an ovary (fruit).
- They are characterized by their flowers, which are the reproductive structures.

2. Characteristics:

- Vascular system (xylem and phloem)
- Seeds are enclosed in an ovary (fruit)
- Reproduction through seeds
- Flowers are the reproductive structures

3. Examples:

- Flowers, trees, and shrubs
- Found in a wide variety of habitats, from deserts to rainforests.

4. Importance:

- They play a crucial role in the ecosystem, serving as food for many animals and insects.
- They also provide habitat and shelter for many species.
- Angiosperms are the source of many of the world's food crops

- **Notes on Cryptograms and Phanerogams:**

Cryptograms:

1. Introduction:

- Cryptograms are a group of lower plants that lack visible flowers and seeds, such as ferns, mosses, liverworts, and hornworts.

2. Characteristics:

- Lack visible flowers and seeds
- Simple structures (no true roots, stems, or leaves)
- Reproduction through spores or spores
- Gametophyte stage is dominant

3. Examples:

- Ferns, mosses, liverworts, and hornworts
- Typically found in moist environments such as forests, swamps, and near water sources.

4. Importance:

- Cryptograms play an important role in soil conservation by preventing erosion and enriching soil.
- They also provide habitat and shelter for many species of insects and animals.

Phanerogams:

1. Introduction:

- Phanerogams are a group of higher plants that have visible flowers and seeds, such as angiosperms and gymnosperms.

2. Characteristics:

- Visible flowers and seeds
- Vascular system (xylem and phloem)
- Reproduction through seeds
- Flowers and cones are the reproductive structures

3. Examples:

- Angiosperms (flowers, trees, and shrubs) and gymnosperms (conifers, cycads, and ginkgos)
- Found in a wide variety of habitats, from deserts to rainforests.

4. Importance:

- Phanerogams play a crucial role in the ecosystem, serving as food for many animals and insects.
- They also provide habitat and shelter for many species.
- Wood from gymnosperms is used for construction, paper production, and fuel.
- Angiosperms are the source of many of the world's food crops.

CHAPTER FOUR

Chapter -4 Animal Kingdom:

1. Introduction:

- The Animal Kingdom is a diverse group of multicellular organisms that are characterized by the absence of cell walls, mobility, and the ability to respond to stimuli.

1. Characteristics:

- Lack of cell walls
- Mobility
- Ability to respond to stimuli
- Heterotrophic (obtain food from other organisms)
- Complex organ systems and tissues

3. Types of animals:

- Invertebrates (animals without backbones) such as sponges, jellyfish, mollusks, arthropods, and echinoderms.
- Vertebrates (animals with backbones) such as fishes, amphibians, reptiles, birds, and mammals.

4. Classification of animals:

- Animals are classified based on characteristics such as body symmetry, presence of coelom, type of skeleton, and mode of reproduction.
- The five-kingdom classification system classifies animals into Monera, Protista, Fungi, Plantae, and Animalia.

5. Importance:

- Animals play a crucial role in the ecosystem, serving as predators, prey, decomposers, and pollinators.
- Many animal species are used as food sources for humans, while others are kept as pets or used for medical research.
- Some animal species serve as indicators of environmental health, helping scientists understand the impacts of human activities on the environment.

6. Endangered species:

- Many animal species are facing extinction due to habitat loss, hunting, and climate change.

- Conservation efforts are underway to protect endangered species and their habitats, including the creation of wildlife reserves and the regulation of hunting.

Characteristics Features of Protozoans, Bryozoans, and Vertebrates:
Protozoans:

1. Introduction:

- Protozoans are single-celled eukaryotic organisms that are classified as members of the kingdom Protista.

2. Characteristics:

- Single-celled
- Eukaryotic (contain a nucleus and other membrane-bound organelles)
- Heterotrophic (obtain food from other organisms)
- Ability to move using pseudopodia, cilia, or flagella
- Simple anatomy

3. Types of Protozoans:

- Amoeboids: move using pseudopodia
- Ciliates: move using cilia
- Flagellates: move using flagella
- Sporozoans: parasites that reproduce through spores or spores

4. Importance:

- Protozoans play a crucial role in the ecosystem, serving as decomposers, parasites, and symbionts.
- Some species of protozoa are used in medical research to study diseases and their treatments.

Bryozoans:

1. Introduction:

- Bryozoans are small, colonial, aquatic animals that are classified as members of the phylum Bryozoa.

2. Characteristics:

- Colonial (consist of many individuals living together)
- Aquatic
- Filter feeders (obtain food by filtering water)
- Simple anatomy
- Reproduce sexually or asexually

3. Types of Bryozoans:

- Freshwater bryozoans
- Marine bryozoans

4. Importance:

- Bryozoans play a role in the ecosystem by filtering water and providing habitat for other aquatic organisms.
- They are also important indicators of environmental health, as changes in bryozoan populations can indicate changes in water quality.

Vertebrates:

1. Introduction:

- Vertebrates are animals with backbones, and are classified as members of the phylum Chordata.

2. Characteristics:

- Backbone
- Vertebral column
- Skull
- Endoskeleton
- Complex organ systems and tissues

3. Types of Vertebrates:

- Fishes
- Amphibians
- Reptiles
- Birds
- Mammals

4. Importance:

- Vertebrates play a crucial role in the ecosystem, serving as predators, prey, and pollinators.
- Many species of vertebrates are used as food sources for humans, while others are kept as pets or used for medical research.
- Vertebrates also serve as indicators of environmental health, helping scientists understand the impacts of human activities on the environment.

Body Symmetry in Kingdom Animalia:

1. Introduction:

- Body symmetry is a characteristic that refers to the shape and arrangement of an animal's body parts.

2. Types of Symmetry:

- Radial symmetry: the body is arranged around a central axis, like a starfish
- Bilateral symmetry: the body is divided into two equal halves along a sagittal plane, like a human.
- Asymmetrical: example sponges that are not able to divide into two equivalent parts in any plane and hence have no appearance of symmetry.

3. Importance:

- Body symmetry is important in animals as it allows for specialized body parts to develop, such as a head and tail, and enables movement and navigation.
- It also affects the way animals feed, moves, and interact with their environment.

Organ Systems in Kingdom Animalia:

1. Introduction:

- An organ system is a group of organs that work together to perform specific functions.

2. Types of Organ Systems in Animals:

- Nervous system: responsible for sensory input, processing information, and coordinating movements
- Circulatory system: responsible for transporting oxygen, nutrients, and hormones throughout the body
- Respiratory system: responsible for exchanging oxygen and carbon dioxide
- Digestive system: responsible for breaking down food and absorbing nutrients
- Urinary system: responsible for removing waste from the body
- Muscular system: responsible for movement
- Skeletal system: provides support and protection
- Integumentary system: protects the body and helps regulate body temperature
- Immune system: protects the body against disease
- Endocrine system: responsible for producing and releasing hormones

Digestive System in Kingdom Animalia:

1. Introduction:

- The digestive system is responsible for breaking down food and absorbing nutrients.

2. Components of the Digestive System:

- Mouth: used for mechanically breaking down food
- Oesophagus: connects the mouth to the stomach
- Stomach: muscular sac that grinds and mixes food
- Small intestine: site of nutrient absorption
- Large intestine: absorbs water and electrolytes, and eliminates waste
- Liver: produces bile to aid in fat digestion
- Pancreas: produces digestive enzymes
- Rectum: stores feces until elimination

3. Types of Digestive system:

v. Complete Digestive System:

- A complete digestive system is a system that includes all of the organs necessary for the breakdown and absorption of food.

- The organs typically found in a complete digestive system include the mouth, esophagus, stomach, small intestine, large intestine, liver, pancreas, and rectum.
- Complete digestive systems are found in animals with more complex digestive systems, such as mammals.

v. Incomplete Digestive System:

- An incomplete digestive system is a system that lacks one or more of the organs necessary for the breakdown and absorption of food.
- For example, some invertebrates have an incomplete digestive system that does not include a separate stomach or small intestine.
- Incomplete digestive systems are found in animals with simpler digestive systems, such as insects and earthworms.

4. Function:

- The digestive system breaks down food into smaller molecules that can be absorbed and used by the body for energy and growth.
- The liver and pancreas also produce enzymes and hormones that aid in digestion and regulation of metabolism.

4. Variation:

- The complexity and anatomy of the digestive system varies among different animal groups, with some having simple, single-chambered systems, while others have multi-chambered, specialized systems.
- The type of diet, such as herbivore, carnivore, or omnivore, can also affect the anatomy and function of the digestive system.

5. Digestive Process:

- The digestive process begins in the mouth where food is mechanically broken down by chewing.
- The chewed food then moves down the esophagus to the stomach where it is mixed with digestive juices and churned.
- The partially digested food then moves into the small intestine where the majority of nutrient absorption takes place.
- The remaining waste material moves into the large intestine where water and electrolytes are absorbed, and the waste material is eliminated through the rectum.

6. Importance:

- The digestive system is critical to the overall health and survival of animals as it allows them to obtain energy and essential nutrients from their food.
- A properly functioning digestive system also helps to prevent disease and maintain the body's balance of fluids and electrolytes.

Circulatory System:

1. Types of Circulatory System:

- Open Circulatory System: Blood flows freely through the body cavity and is not enclosed in vessels. Found in invertebrates such as insects and crustaceans.
- Closed Circulatory System: Blood is enclosed in vessels and circulates through the body in a closed loop. Found in vertebrates and some invertebrates.

2. Functions:

- The circulatory system is responsible for transporting oxygen, nutrients, and hormones throughout the body.
- It also helps to regulate body temperature and maintain the body's balance of fluids and electrolytes.

Important questions and answers on <u>Chapter 1 "The Living World"</u>

Q1. What is the definition of biodiversity?

Ans1. Biodiversity refers to the variety of living organisms present in a particular ecosystem or on the planet, including species, genetic diversity, and ecosystem diversity.

Q2. What are the major categories of biodiversity?

Ans2. The major categories of biodiversity include species diversity, genetic diversity, and ecosystem diversity.

Q3. What is the significance of biodiversity in the ecosystem?

Ans3. Biodiversity is important for maintaining the health and stability of ecosystems, as well as for providing a variety of benefits to human societies, such as food, medicine, and ecosystem services such as pollination and water purification.

Q4. What are the threats to biodiversity?

Ans4. The major threats to biodiversity include habitat loss, climate change, pollution, overexploitation, and invasive species.

Q5. What is the difference between endemic and exotic species?

Ans5. Endemic species are those that are found only in a particular geographic region, while exotic species are those that have been introduced to a region from outside its natural range.

Q6. What are the major biomes of the world?

Ans6. The world's major biomes include tropical rainforests, deserts, grasslands, temperate forests, boreal forests, and tundra.

Q7. What is the importance of conservation of biodiversity?

Ans7. Conservation of biodiversity is important for maintaining the health and stability of ecosystems, as well as for preserving the many benefits that biodiversity provides to human societies. Conservation also helps to protect endangered species from extinction, and to maintain the natural beauty and cultural significance of natural areas.

Q8. What is the difference between in situ and ex situ conservation?

Ans8. In situ conservation refers to the conservation of species and ecosystems in their natural habitats, while ex situ conservation involves the conservation of species and genetic diversity outside of their natural habitats, such as in zoos, botanical gardens, and seed banks.

Q9. What is the role of the International Union for Conservation of Nature (IUCN) in biodiversity conservation?

Ans9. The IUCN is a global organization that works to conserve biodiversity by providing scientific expertise, promoting the sustainable use of natural resources, and developing policies and programs to protect endangered species and ecosystems.

Q10. What are the major international agreements and protocols related to biodiversity conservation?

Ans10. The major international agreements and protocols related to biodiversity conservation include the Convention on Biological Diversity, the Cartagena Protocol on Biosafety, and the Nagoya Protocol on Access to Genetic Resources and the Fair and Equitable Sharing of Benefits Arising from their Utilization.

Important questions and answers on Chapter 2 Biological Classification

Q1. What is the biological classification of organisms?

Ans1. Biological classification is the process of grouping organisms into hierarchical categories based on their shared characteristics.

Q2. What are the advantages of the classification of organisms?

Ans2. The classification of organisms helps us to better understand the diversity of life on Earth, identify relationships between different species, and to develop a system for naming and organizing living organisms.

Q3. What is taxonomy?

Ans3. Taxonomy is the branch of biology that deals with the identification, classification, and naming of living organisms.

Q4. What are the different levels of classification in the Linnaean system?

Ans4. The different levels of classification in the Linnaean system are domain, kingdom, phylum, class, order, family, genus, and species.

Q5. What is the difference between natural and artificial classification?

Ans5. Natural classification is based on the natural relationships between organisms, while artificial classification is based on arbitrary criteria such as physical appearance or utility.

Q6. What is the basis of classification in Whittaker's five-kingdom classification system?

Ans6. Whittaker's five-kingdom classification system is based on the criteria of cell structure, mode of nutrition, and body organization. The five kingdoms are Monera, Protista, Fungi, Plantae, and Animalia.

Q7. What is the difference between prokaryotic and eukaryotic cells?

Ans7. Prokaryotic cells are cells that lack a true nucleus and other membrane-bound organelles, while eukaryotic cells have a true nucleus and membrane-bound organelles.

Q8. What is the significance of binomial nomenclature?

Ans8. Binomial nomenclature is a system of naming living organisms using a two-part Latin name, consisting of the genus name and the species name. This system allows for a standardized and universally recognized system of naming and organizing living organisms.

Q9. What is the importance of cladistics in biological classification?

Ans9. Cladistics is a method of biological classification that groups organisms based on their shared characteristics and evolutionary relationships. It helps to provide a more accurate and natural classification system that reflects the true relationships between different species.

Q10. What is the difference between analogical and homologous structures?

Ans10. Analogical structures are structures that have a similar function but have evolved independently in different species, while homologous structures are structures that have a similar evolutionary origin but may have different functions in different species. The presence of homologous structures provides evidence of evolutionary relationships between different species.

Important Question on Chapter 3 Plant Kingdom

Q1. What are the different modes of nutrition in plants?

Ans1. Plants can have autotrophic, heterotrophic or mixotrophic modes of nutrition. Autotrophic plants are those that produce their food through photosynthesis, while heterotrophic plants rely on other organisms for their food. Mixotrophic plants have both autotrophic and heterotrophic modes of nutrition.

Q2. What are the differences between gymnosperms and angiosperms?

Ans2. Gymnosperms are plants that have naked seeds, meaning their seeds are not enclosed within a fruit. Angiosperms, on the other hand, are plants that have seeds enclosed within a fruit. Gymnosperms also do not have flowers, while angiosperms do.

Q3. What is alternation of generations?

Ans3. Alternation of generations is a reproductive process in plants in which there are two distinct phases, one haploid (n) and one diploid (2n). The haploid phase is called the gametophyte, and the diploid phase is called the sporophyte. In alternation of generations, the gametophyte produces gametes through mitosis, which then fuse to form a zygote. The zygote develops into a sporophyte through mitosis, which then produces spores through meiosis. The spores develop into gametophytes, and the cycle starts again.

Q4. What is the importance of Bryophytes in the ecosystem?

Ans4. Bryophytes are important in the ecosystem for several reasons. They help to prevent soil erosion, provide habitats for small animals and insects, and contribute to nutrient cycling. They are also important indicators of environmental health, as they are sensitive to changes in air and water quality.

Q5. What is vegetative propagation?

Ans5. Vegetative propagation is a type of asexual reproduction in plants, where new plants are produced from non-reproductive plant parts, such as leaves, stems, and roots. This method is commonly used in horticulture and agriculture to produce identical copies of plants that have desirable traits.

Q6. What is the significance of seeds in the life cycle of plants?

Ans6. Seeds are important in the life cycle of plants because they are the means by which plants reproduce and spread. Seeds contain the embryo of the plant, along with stored food and a protective outer layer. This allows the plant to survive in harsh conditions and to disperse to new locations. Seeds are also important in agriculture, as they are used to grow crops.

Q7. What are the different types of roots in plants?

Ans7. There are three main types of roots in plants: taproots, fibrous roots, and adventitious roots. Taproots are a large, central root that grows deep into the ground, while fibrous roots are a network of small roots that spread out near the surface of the soil. Adventitious roots are roots that arise from non-root tissues, such as stems or leaves.

Q8. What is the difference between monocots and dicots?

Ans8. Monocots and dicots are two types of flowering plants. Monocots have one cotyledon (seed leaf) in their embryo, while dicots have two. Monocots also have parallel leaf veins, while dicots have branching leaf veins. Monocots have flower parts in multiples of three, while dicots have flower parts in multiples of four or five. Finally, monocots have fibrous roots, while dicots have taproots.

Q9. What is the function of leaves in plants?

Ans9. Leaves are the primary organs of photosynthesis in plants.

They are responsible for absorbing light energy and converting it into chemical energy in the form of glucose through the process of photosynthesis. Leaves also play a role in transpiration, where water is lost from the plant through small pores in the leaves called stomata. Additionally, leaves are involved in gas exchange, as they take in carbon dioxide for photosynthesis and release oxygen through the stomata.

Q10. What is the importance of flowers in the life cycle of plants?

Ans10. Flowers are the reproductive structures of plants, and are responsible for the production of seeds. Flowers contain both male and female reproductive structures, allowing for fertilization to occur and for the development of seeds. Flowers also play a role in pollination, where pollen is transferred from the male to the female reproductive structures, allowing for fertilization to occur. This can occur through a variety of methods, such as wind, water, or the actions of animals. Flowers are also important in horticulture and agriculture, as they are used to produce fruits and vegetables.

Important Questions/Answers Chapter-4 Animal Kingdom

Q1. What are the different types of symmetry in animals?

Ans1. There are three types of symmetry in animals: bilateral symmetry, radial symmetry, and asymmetry. Bilateral symmetry is when an animal can be divided into two identical halves by a single plane, while radial symmetry is when an animal can be divided into identical halves by multiple planes. Asymmetry is when an animal has no symmetry.

Q2. What is the difference between coelomate, acoelomate and pseudocoelomate animals?

Ans2. Coelomate animals have a true body cavity called a coelom, which is completely lined by mesoderm. Acoelomate animals lack a coelom, filling their body cavity with mesodermal tissue. Pseudocoelomate animals have a body cavity called a pseudocoelom, which is only partially lined by mesoderm.

Q3. What is the importance of phylum Arthropoda in the animal kingdom?

Ans3. Phylum Arthropoda is the largest phylum in the animal kingdom and includes insects, spiders, and crustaceans. Arthropods are important for a variety of reasons, including their role in pollination, their use as a food source, and their role in maintaining ecological balance. Arthropods also serve as important vectors for the transmission of diseases.

Q4. What is the difference between endothermic and ectothermic animals?

Ans4. Endothermic animals are those that can regulate their body temperature internally, such as mammals and birds. Ectothermic animals are those that rely on external sources of heat to regulate their body temperatures, such as reptiles and amphibians.

Q5. What is the significance of the excretory system in animals?

Ans5. The excretory system is responsible for removing waste products from the body, including nitrogenous wastes such as ammonia and urea. This helps to maintain proper fluid and electrolyte balance and prevents the accumulation of toxic substances in the body.

Q6. What is the difference between a complete and incomplete digestive system?

Ans6. A complete digestive system is one in which the digestive tract has two openings, a mouth, and an anus, and food travels through the digestive system in one direction. An incomplete digestive system has only one opening, and food enters and leaves the body through the same opening.

Q7. What is the function of the nervous system in animals?

Ans7. The nervous system is responsible for transmitting and processing information throughout the body. This includes the senses, such as vision and hearing, as well as controlling movements and behaviours. The nervous system also plays a role in regulating physiological processes such as heart rate and respiration.

Q8. What is the significance of the circulatory system in animals?

Ans8. The circulatory system is responsible for transporting nutrients, gases, and waste products throughout the body. It helps to maintain proper fluid balance and plays a role in regulating body temperature. The circulatory system also plays a key role in the immune response, helping to transport immune cells and antibodies to fight infections.

Q9. What is the difference between asexual and sexual reproduction in animals?

Ans9. Asexual reproduction is when offspring are produced without the involvement of gametes, and the offspring are genetically identical to the parent. Sexual reproduction is when offspring are produced through the fusion of gametes, and the offspring have a combination of genetic material from both parents.

Q10. What is the significance of the respiratory system in animals?

Ans10. The respiratory system is responsible for exchanging gases between the body and the environment. It helps to bring in oxygen, which is necessary for cellular respiration, and remove carbon dioxide, which is a waste product of cellular respiration. The respiratory system also helps to regulate the pH of the body and plays a role in the sense of smell.

Q11. What is the difference between invertebrates and vertebrates?

Ans11. Invertebrates are animals that lack a backbone, while vertebrates are animals that have a backbone. Invertebrates make up the majority of animal species, and include insects, worms, and molluscs, while vertebrates include fish, birds, mammals, and reptiles.

Q12. What is the role of the digestive system in animals?

Ans12. The digestive system is responsible for breaking down food into its component molecules, which can be absorbed by the body for use in cellular respiration and other physiological processes. The digestive system includes organs such as the mouth, oesophagus, stomach, small intestine, and large intestine, and is aided by accessory organs such as the liver and pancreas.

Q13. What is the significance of the immune system in animals?

Ans13. The immune system is responsible for defending the body against infections and diseases. It includes a variety of specialized cells and molecules, such as white blood cells and antibodies, which work together to identify and eliminate pathogens such as bacteria and viruses. The immune system also plays a role in the healing process, helping to repair damaged tissues.

Q14. What is the significance of phylum Chordata in the animal kingdom?

Ans14. Phylum Chordata is a diverse group of animals that includes vertebrates as well as some invertebrates. Chordates are characterized by the presence of a notochord, a dorsal nerve cord, and pharyngeal slits, which are important features in embryonic development. Chordates play a critical role in the ecosystem and include animals such as fish, birds, and mammals.

Q15. What is the difference between a herbivore, carnivore, and omnivore?

Ans15. A herbivore is an animal that primarily eats plants, while a carnivore is an animal that primarily eats meat. An omnivore is an animal that eats both plants and animals. The type of diet an animal has is often related to the type of digestive system and teeth the animal has, as well as its habitat and evolutionary history.

Dear CBSE Class 11 Book Readers,

I would like to take this opportunity to express my sincere gratitude for choosing my book as your academic resource. It is my pleasure to know that my book has been a helpful tool in your studies and has aided in your academic growth.

I would like to extend my best wishes to all the CBSE Class 11 students for their future academic endeavors. May you continue to strive for excellence and achieve all your goals.

Thank you once again for choosing my book as your academic resource.

Best regards,

Monica

Printed by Libri Plureos GmbH in Hamburg,
Germany